Scripture quotations, unless otherwise noted, are taken from the HOLY BIBLE, NEW INTERNATIONAL VERSION®. NIV®. Copyright © 1973, 1978, 1984 by International Bible Society. Used by permission of Zondervan Publishing House. All rights reserved.

Scripture quotations marked KJV are taken from the King James Version of the Bible.

Poems by Wanda Royer are copyrighted and used by permission.

Published by Barbour Publishing, Inc., P.O. Box 719, Uhrichsville, Ohio 44683, www.barbourbooks.com

Member of the
Evangelical Christian
Publishers Association

Printed in China.
5 4 3 2 1

The Greatest Gift

REBECCA GERMANY

The greatest gift was....?

A baby?

And is it true?
And is it true,
This most tremendous tale of all,
Seen in a stained-glass window's hue,
A Baby in an ox's stall?
The Maker of the stars and sea
Became a Child on earth for me?

Sir John Betjeman

Gold,
incense,
and
myrrh?

The magi, as you know, were wise men—

wonderfully wise men who brought gifts

to the Babe in the manger.

They invented the art of giving

Christmas presents.

O. HENRY

On coming to the house, they saw the child

with his mother Mary,

and they bowed down and worshiped him.

Then they opened their treasures and presented him

with gifts of gold and of incense and of myrrh.

MATTHEW 2:11

A wonderful holiday?

It's Christmastime!

It's Christmastime!

I'm so happy it's Christmastime!

Hearts are happy and songs are gay

God's Son was born on Christmas Day.

WANDA ROYER

Peace on earth will come to stay,

When we live Christmas

every day.

HELEN STEINER RICE

The Greatest Gift Is

Love!

Love was born Yesterday
Love lives Today
Love reigns Forever

When we celebrate Christmas
we are celebrating that amazing time when the Word
that shouted all the galaxies into being,
limited all power, and for love of us came to us
in the powerless body of a human baby.

MADELEINE L'ENGLE

The love of God is like the Amazon River
flowing down to water one daisy.

AUTHOR UNKNOWN

Many waters cannot quench love;
rivers cannot wash it away.
If one were to give all the wealth of his house for love,
it would be utterly scorned.

SONG OF SONGS 8:7

Yesterday

For God so loved the world

that he gave his one and only Son,

that whoever believes in him

shall not perish but have eternal life.

JOHN 3:16

Love came down at Christmas,
Love all lovely, Love Divine;
Love was born at Christmas;
Star and angels gave the sign.

CHRISTINA ROSSETTI

Good news from heaven the angels bring,
Glad tidings to the earth they sing:
To us this day a child is given,
To crown us with the joy of heaven.

MARTIN LUTHER

Jesus was God spelling
himself out in language humanity could understand.

S. D. GORDON

He is the image of the invisible God,

the firstborn over all creation.

COLOSSIANS 1:15

[In the person of Christ] a man
has not become God; God has become man.

CYRIL OF ALEXANDRIA

Jesus did not come

to make God's love possible,

but to make God's

love visible.

AUTHOR UNKNOWN

*H*e came in complete human form
to meet a universal need in a way that is
adequate for all times and places
and is without parallel or substitute.

H. D. LEWIS

Christ was not half a God and half a man;
he was perfectly God and perfectly man.

JAMES STALKER

*A*lthough Christ was God, he took flesh;
and having been made man,
he remained what he was, God.

ORIGEN

Our Lord

took a body like ours and lived as a man
in order that those who had refused to recognize him
in his superintendence and captaincy of the whole
universe might come to recognize from the works he
did here below in the body, that what dwelt in this
body was the Word of God.

ATHANASIUS

On Christmas Day

two thousand years ago,
the birth of a tiny baby in an
obscure village in the Middle East
was God's supreme triumph of good over evil.

CHARLES COLSON

More light than we can learn,

More wealth than we can treasure,

More love than we can earn,

More peace than we can measure,

Because one Child is born.

AUTHOR UNKNOWN

Love's mark on history. . .

All history is incomprehensible

without Christ.

ERNEST RENAN

The birth of the baby Jesus stands as the most significant
event in all history, because it has meant the pouring into
a sick world of the healing medicine of love which has
transformed all manner of hearts for almost two thousand years. . . .

GEORGE MATTHEW ADAMS

The simple record of three short years of active
life has done more to regenerate and to soften mankind,
than all the disquisitions of philosophers
and than all the exhortations of moralists.

W. E. H. LECKY

After 1900 years, Jesus Christ still counts for more
in human life than any other man that ever lived.

DEAN INGE

*A*s the centuries pass the evidence is accumulating that,
measured by His effect on history,
Jesus is the most influential life ever lived on this planet.

KENNETH SCOTT LATOURETTE

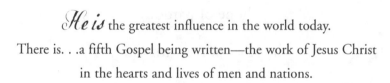

He is the greatest influence in the world today.
There is. . .a fifth Gospel being written—the work of Jesus Christ
in the hearts and lives of men and nations.

W. H. GRIFFITH THOMAS

*J*esus Christ will still be important for mankind
two or three thousand years hence.

H. G. WELLS

A Cross Built by Love

The Christmas message is that there is

hope for a ruined humanity—

hope of pardon,

hope of peace with God,

hope of glory—

because at the Father's will Jesus Christ became poor,

and was born in a stable so that thirty years later

He might hang on a cross.

J. I. PACKER

But he was pierced for our transgressions,
he was crushed for our iniquities;
the punishment that brought us peace was upon him,
and by his wounds we are healed.

ISAIAH 53:5

One drop of Christ's blood is worth
more than heaven and earth.

MARTIN LUTHER

Nails could not have kept Jesus on the cross
had love not held Him there.

AUTHOR UNKNOWN

But God demonstrates his own love for us in this:

While we were still sinners,

Christ died for us.

ROMANS 5:8

He came to pay a debt he did not owe,

because we owed a debt we could not pay.

AUTHOR UNKNOWN

Christ's blood is heaven's key.

THOMAS BROOKS

There is a green hill far away,
Without a city wall,
Where the dear Lord was crucified,
Who died to save us all.

C. F. ALEXANDER

Jesus of Nazareth, without money and arms,
conquered more millions than
Alexander, Caesar, Mahomet, and Napoleon.

PHILIP SCHAFF

Jesus Christ's claim of divinity is
the most serious claim anyone ever made.
Everything about Christianity hinges on
His incarnation, crucifixion, and resurrection.
That's what Christmas, Good Friday, and Easter are all about.

LUIS PALAU

Bethlehem and Golgotha, the Manger and the Cross,
the Birth and the Death, must always be seen together.

J. SIDLOW BAXTER

God proved his love on the cross.

When Christ hung, and bled, and died,

it was God saying to the world—

I love you.

BILLY GRAHAM

Today

What can I give him,

Poor as I am?

If I were a shepherd,

I would bring a lamb,

If I were a Wise Man,

I would do my part—

Yet what I can, I give Him,

Give my heart.

CHRISTINA ROSSETTI

Man of Sorrows! what a name
For the Son of God, who came
Ruined sinners to reclaim!
Hallelujah, what a Savior!

PHILIP PAUL BLISS

Salvation is found in no one else,

for there is no other name under heaven given

to men by which we must be saved.

ACTS 4:12

*T*he Early Christians believed that salvation is
a gift from God but that God gives his gift to whomever he chooses.
And he chooses to give it to those who love and obey him.

D. W. BERCOT

Anyone can devise a plan
by which good people go to heaven.
Only God can devise a plan whereby sinners,
which are His enemies, can go to heaven.

LEWIS SPERRY CHAFER

*F*or it is by grace you have been saved,
through faith—and this not from yourselves,
it is the gift of God.

EPHESIANS 2:8

Behold, I stand at the door, and knock:
>   if any man hear my voice, and open the door,
>   I will come in to him, and will sup with him,
>   and he with me.

REVELATION 3:20 KJV

This day and your life are God's gifts to you:
>   so give thanks and be joyful always!

JIM BEGGS

Every good and perfect gift
    is from above,
coming down from the Father
    of the heavenly lights,
who does not change
    like shifting shadows.

JAMES 1:17

*G*ive ear and come to me;
hear me, that your soul may live.
I will make an everlasting covenant with you,
my faithful love promised to David.

ISAIAH 55:3

Forever

Born thy people to deliver,

Born a child, and yet a king,

Born to reign in us forever,

Now thy gracious kingdom bring.

CHARLES WESLEY

Rejoice,

that the immortal God is born,

so that mortal man may live in eternity.

JOHN HUSS

~⌇~

Christ's words are permanent

value because of His person;

they endure because He endures.

W. H. GRIFFITH THOMAS

In my Father's house are many rooms;

if it were not so,

I would have told you.

I am going there to prepare a place for you.

And if I go and prepare a place for you,

I will come back and take you to be with me

that you also may be where I am.

JOHN 14:2–3

One day we will meet beside the river and

our Lord will dry every tear.

For now, we must live in the joy of that promise

and recall that for every generation life is hard,

but God is faithful.

BODIE THOENE

Faith is not knowing what the future holds,
but knowing who holds the future.

AUTHOR UNKNOWN

Now faith is being sure of what

we hope for and certain of what we do not see.

HEBREWS 11:1

And surely I am with you always,
to the very end of the age.

MATTHEW 28:20

I rejoice in the hope of that glory to be revealed, for it is no uncertain glory that we look for. Our hope is not hung upon such an untwisted thread as, "I imagine so," or "It is likely," but the cable, the strong tow of our fastened anchor, is the oath and promise of Him who is eternal verity. Our salvation is fastened with God's own hand, and with Christ's own strength, to the strong stake of God's unchangeable nature.

SAMUEL RUTHERFORD

Jesus Christ is the same yesterday and today and forever.

HEBREWS 13:8

"*Behold,* I am coming soon! My reward is with me,
and I will give to everyone according to what he has done.
I am the Alpha and the Omega, the First and the Last,
the Beginning and the End."

REVELATION 22:12–13

*Give thanks to the Lord,
for he is good;
his love endures forever.*

PSALM 118:1

'*Twas* love divine that Holy night

That came to make this dark world light.

He came to us from Heav'n above

To teach us how to live with love.

I'll serve Him till the end of time.

I'll tell the world of love divine;

True peace is mine——let come what may;

O! I'm so happy for Christmas Day.

WANDA ROYER

Are you willing to believe that love

is the strongest thing in the world—

stronger than hate, stronger than evil,

stronger than death—

and that the blessed life which began

in Bethlehem nineteen hundred years ago is

the image and brightness of the Eternal Love?

Then you can keep Christmas.

HENRY VAN DYKE